Alignment for Assignment

THE PERPETUAL SHIFT

ALIGNMENT FOR ASSIGNMENT

THE PERPETUAL SHIFT

SEAN S. WALSH
Foreword by Martha Munizzi

Wasteland Press
Shelbyville, KY USA
www.wastelandpress.net

Alignment For Assignment: The Perpetual Shift
By Sean S. Walsh

Copyright © 2008 Sean S. Walsh
ALL RIGHTS RESERVED

First Printing – August 2008
ISBN: 978-1-60047-144-5

Cover design by "O" Design Factory
Photographer Daniel Sutton

NO PART OF THIS BOOK MAY BE REPRODUCED IN ANY FORM, BY PHOTOCOPYING OR BY ANY ELECTRONIC OR MECHANICAL MEANS, INCLUDING INFORMATION STORAGE OR RETRIEVAL SYSTEMS, WITHOUT PERMISSION IN WRITING FROM THE COPYRIGHT OWNER/AUTHOR.

Unless otherwise indicated all scripture has been used from the HOLY BIBLE, NEW INTERNATIONAL VERSION®. Copyright © 1973, 1978, 1984 International Bible Society. Used by permission of Zondervan. All rights reserved.

Printed in the U.S.A.

Dedication

I want to dedicate this book to one of the greatest gifts God has given to me...my lovely wife, Kim. Thank you so much for your dedication and determination. It's great to know that you are a supernatural and natural support to the call of God on my life. Most of all I am thankful for our friendship.

I would also like to dedicate this book to all my friends and all the people who have supported me through their prayers and finances. May God richly bless you!

Special Thanks

I would like to say a special thanks to Martha Munizzi and Apostle Michael Pitts for believing in me and the call of God on my life. It is such a special blessing to me to know that great people of God like you were willing to endorse my first book. May you walk under an open heaven and receive God's best!

Foreword

I've had the joy of knowing Sean and his wife, Kim, for the past four years. During this time they have been such a blessing and encouragement to me personally, and to my family. I'm so excited to be a witness to the vision and the destiny the Lord has for this special couple. Sean's book, *Alignment for Assignment*, is a prophetic word to the Church today.

As Christians it is time we truly understand our authority, time to take our position in the world and time to embrace personal responsibility for integrity. This book reminds us that we are responsible to continue to do the 'right thing!' God is responsible for promotion…

Alignment for Assignment will help us all understand that God has a greater plan that is at work in the world. It doesn't matter what your life looks like right now – it doesn't matter what the situations around you say. God remains steadfast, true and in control. I've sensed in my spirit such a great stirring. It's time to move away from tradition or religious ways…

Remember – it's a new season! Shifts are in the air!

Martha Munizzi
Award Winning Singer/Songwriter
International Worship Leader

Praise for *Alignment for Assignment*

"Sean Walsh is a dear servant of God who understands placement, alignment, assignment, and promotion. The words you will read in this, his first book, are not theory or rhetoric. They have, however, been proved out through the fire of testing and the crucible of time in his own life. Read it and be blessed."

Apostle Michael S. Pitts
Cornerstone Church Toledo, Ohio

"I have personally known Sean Walsh since August of 1996. Sean is not only a man of God but also a man of integrity. He has a great gift in the realm of the Prophetic; I know this first hand as he has prophesied over my life and ministry and every word that proceeded out of his mouth has come to pass. He has always maintained his walk and witness as a true Christian, and has managed to have a life of divine order and accountability. This general in the Kingdom of God is truly a voice of power for this end time harvest of souls."

Jason A. Fredenburg
Senior Pastor of Harvest of Victory Church
Ann Arbor, Michigan

"I have seen Sean grow in leaps and bounds in the ten years I have known him. He has walked through the fire, and withstood the test. He carries an anointing which rips the covers off the plans of the enemy, releasing an anointing to refresh, restore and revolutionize the Body of Christ. Words of power flow out of First Watch Ministries with power and pinpoint accuracy."

Pastor Brian Gallardo
World of Truth Ministries
Kansas City, Missouri

"Through this book Minister Sean Walsh has not only created a vivid picture of the next Kingdom shift, but he has prophetically contributed to its definition and development. Alignment for Assignment is a wise addition to the library of any person who does not merely want to witness the next move of God, but wants to participate."

Apostle Angela Kittrell
Emmanuel Faith Ministries
Fredericksburg, Virginia

"I believe that Sean has a supernatural anointing on his life that allows him to lock his faith with yours, tying into God's supernatural source to create a supernatural harvest that you have been waiting for. This is not for the weak of heart or for those who want to plateau in their walk with God. This is for those who want to see God's fire, who want to touch His power, who want to sense His presence, and who want to be enveloped by His Glory. I believe that Sean, with the anointing and insights that he brings from God, will lead you into the greatest life changing experience you have only dreamed of. Are you ready?"

Minister Lonnie Peterson
Indianapolis, Indiana

Word from My Pastor

"Wow!! What more can be said about the precise prophetic timing of this book. Sean has tuned his ear to the voice of the Holy Spirit and this book releases incredible revelation for every believer who is serious about the "NOW" of God. Open your spirit as you read and be transformed .... changed...shifted... by the same anointing in which this was penned. I know Sean and I know he has hit the mark with this book; it is eye-opening and life changing."

Apostle Kevin Mihlfeld
Strong Tower Ministries
Fredericksburg, Virginia

Word from My Wife

"The first time I ever saw Sean, I knew he was marked by God. Little did I know that two years later we would be married and on an incredible journey together for the Kingdom. Sean has the ability to unlock new dimensions in the Spirit through prayer and prophetic proclamation. God has given him incredible insight into His Kingdom along with discernment and prophetic accuracy, which he neither takes lightly nor abuses. Many people who have been ministered to by Sean have affirmed and confirmed his prophetic accuracy. Considering the greatness that is on Sean's life and how God uses him, it would be easy for him to become super-spiritual, but Sean still has the ability to be real, relevant and funny! I'm so proud to see the revelation that God placed in Sean's spirit finally be birthed into a manuscript. This book will challenge you and bless you. To my husband – you owe me big time for putting up with you during all of this!"

Pastor Kimberly Walsh
Strong Tower Ministries
Fredericksburg, Virginia

Why I Wrote This Book

In the beginning of the year 2005, the Lord began to speak with me concerning the prophetic word "shift." A few months later, He spoke to me on a greater level, perspective and dimension than I had ever heard before and He began to download this powerful revelation you are about to read. He began to show me that not only are things as we know them going to shift and change but also on His agenda is the restoration of the Five Fold Ministry to the local church. He also showed me that the spiritual shift that had begun in 2005 was not only for that year, but was just the beginning of things to come. As He was developing this greater dimension of the shift within me, I began to realize this revelation was not just for me only. However, I wasn't sure how to get it out there. After preaching a message in line with the theme of this revelation, the Lord impressed upon me to add to the message and put it into a book format.

I truly believe that the best days are just ahead for the Body of Christ. I believe that great revelations are and will be coming forth for the greater development of the Body. We are being propelled head first into greater destiny, greater victory, greater manifestations of miracles, and greater manifestations of the Holy Ghost.

I am telling you the future is going to be bigger, better, and brighter, on both personal levels and international levels, than what we have experienced before. Our past as the Body of Christ is just that – the past. It's over! A new day is dawning so get ready!

Table of Contents

Introduction		1
Chapter 1:	Time Is Up!	7
Chapter 2:	A Renewed Position of Authority	17
Chapter 3:	Ready, Set, Shift!	25
Chapter 4:	It's Time for More	31
Chapter 5:	The All-At-Once Church	39
Chapter 6:	The Breath of Revival	45
Chapter 7:	The Assignment	51
Closing Comments		56
Salvation		57
Additional Scriptural Examples of Kingdom Shifts		59

Introduction

It's time to get excited and know that our best days are ahead. I know you've heard this plenty of times – but it is truer now than ever before. We serve a God who is bringing us from glory to glory. The only way we can't move ahead is to reject this next move of God.

My goal in writing this book is not only to give the Body of Christ a snapshot of what *is* happening right now, but also what is *about* to happen within the Body as a whole. I also would like to point out that I did not intend this to be a difficult read with a bunch of flowery words. My assignment is to simply lay out the plan of God.

There is a small section/group in the Body of Christ, which in preacher terms is called the remnant – a church that is within the church. This remnant has been undergoing a major shift that will soon be manifested throughout the Body as a whole. Let me explain what I mean about the church within a church, or the remnant so to speak. This remnant consists of the saints who are not just satisfied with going to church when it is convenient for them, or whenever they need a quick fix for their issues. This group of people is willing to pay a price, to go the extra mile – not just once – but every time it's required. They are those people who are at church every time the doors are open, not because they have to be but because they want to be.

This major shift that has started among the remnant is very much like a world altering, life changing tsunami. Tsunamis are created by an inner shifting of the earth's plates, which is better known as an earthquake. Once the inner plates have shifted under the ocean, this immediately sends waves running at top speed to the nearest area of land. This is known as a ripple effect. Better said – for every action there is a reaction. So, as the shifting of the inner part of the Body of Christ manifests, this will in turn be felt like shock waves throughout the whole Body of Christ.

In January of 2005, I was praying in my office. This was just a short time after that terrible tsunami hit the islands of Asia, and the world was still in a state of shock. It was around 10:00 a.m. and just before our Sunday morning service. I could feel that the atmosphere was fully charged and that God was about to do amazing things in our midst that day.

Little did I know that God was about to open my spirit wide and pour into me an amazing revelation. Right in the middle of praying, God shared with me a vision and what I began to see was truly wild! In this vision I saw almost a replay of the recent tsunami that had just devastated parts of Asia and Africa. I saw great waves swelling, swirling, and tossing a countless number of people and destroying massive buildings and structures.

As this vision unfolded, I can remember thinking, "What is this, Lord?" He quickly answered me saying, "Sean, don't look at these as waves of destruction, but look at them as waves of my glory." (I must let you know that God does not get glory out of the destruction of His creation. He simply used this as an illustration to give me in a vision, a revelation.) I believe that God used the magnitude of that Asian event to show me what it will be like as He releases one of the greatest anointings and shifts in the Body of Christ.

In other words, things as we know them today are about to change to such a degree that there will be no resemblance to how things used to be, to the effect that we will have no previous experience or move of the Holy Spirit to compare it to. We are about to experience God on greater levels than we ever have before. We will see things like we have never seen manifesting in the Church as a whole.

As I stated before, the amazing thing about this revelation is that, in order for there to be a tsunami on the surface of this planet, there first has to be a shift in the inner parts. The Body of Christ is undergoing an internal shift and a major component of that is the process of realizing who we are and what we are here to do.

The Year 2005 was a year of many significant words and adjustments from God. The most prominent, which will affect years to come – and even generations to come – was the prophetic word "Shift."

God always has and always will work in shifts. The Spirit of God has moved in shifts from the beginning of time. I find that God has always had His greatest creation – man – right in the middle of every shift. I am a firm believer that in order for God to shift things on this earth, He's going to have to use a man. One of the most powerful forces that man carries, whether he chooses to or not, is the power of influence! Influence is the ability that man has to emanate the Spirit of God and the authority of God here on this earth.

The Body of Christ started out with great influence and, unfortunately, we have lost the strength of that influence over the years. Instead of having answers to problems, we have become the problem in the way we walk around acting like the world owes us something, instead of us owing them the opportunity to hear and experience the gospel. But I have great news – things are shifting! The Body of Christ is coming out of obscurity and the position of being a negative representation of the Kingdom of God.

Over the next few chapters, I want to share with you what God has shared with me – this prophetic revelation of the many ways the Body of Christ will be shifting in the days and years ahead. God is bringing us into *alignment* so that we can fulfill our *assignment*, because a body that is out of alignment does not have the full capability to function at its maximum potential.

Chapter One

Time Is Up!

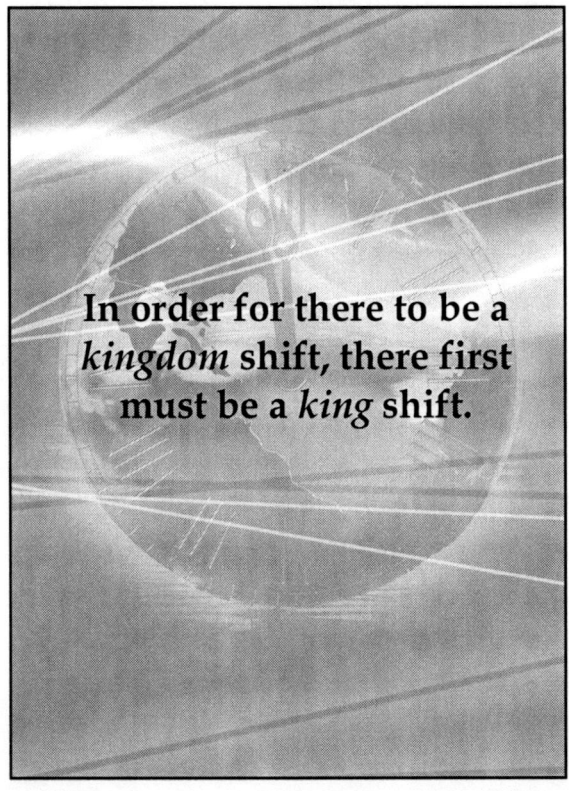

In order for there to be a *kingdom* shift, there first must be a *king* shift.

Daniel 2:21

He changes times and seasons;
He sets up kings and deposes them.

The Book of Daniel says it well, *"He sets up kings and deposes them."* I have an announcement to make: God is putting His foot down and removing kings (preachers, politicians, local and government officials and other influential people) who are not willing to exercise Godly influence or bless their region or place of authority. God is removing kings who have been occupying an office/position and have been doing nothing with it – the ones who have been a liability rather than an asset.

I believe that the people who are currently in authority will be judged in the upcoming Kingdom shift; those whose tendencies are wicked and who are not willing to honor God are about to be replaced. **In order for there to be a *kingdom* shift, there first must be a *king* shift.** A kingdom carries no greater power than its king. A kingdom can rise no higher than the level of its king.

A king is the one who holds the authority to declare the decree, the law of the land. The Book of Ecclesiastes, Chapter 8:4 KJV, says, *"Where the word of a King is, there is power."* That land is subject to the word of that king and can only produce as it is commissioned to produce with the release of the king's decree. The king is the one who holds the ability to oppress and withhold blessings from his kingdom, or release blessings and bring life to his domain.

A kingdom either fails or has great success in its region according to its ability to influence that region. It's all up to the king to decide the degree to which he wants the region to produce. And so it is with the Church. We, the Church, must control our regions (our strategic locations) spiritually and politically with the tool called "influence." Every church has been assigned to a region and is responsible for what does or does not take place within that region. For example, have you ever seen a church that has tried to do something productive in its own region and it has flopped? Well, this is simply due to the fact that this church has not taken the time to get to know its region, or the flow and lifestyle of the people they are ministering to. If churches would get the mindset that they must first dominate with Kingdom authority their own regions before pursuing other regions, they would carry a greater influence. I am a firm believer that if you would first bring change to the people of your community, then that force of influence will affect other communities and begin to spread outward to influence regions.

As an FYI – it would do churches well to discern the prevailing spirit over their area so they can target that spirit with prayer and tear it down. Also, learn from other churches but don't use cookie cutter methods for reaching your community. Tap into what God is doing in this great shifting of the Spirit, see how it applies to your area, and watch God do great things.

I am sure we can think of a person who holds some level or position of authority – whether on a large scale, such as a dignitary of a country, or all the way down to the local authority of a small town – who does not have much of a Godly influence or even cares to exercise the Godly influence that he does have. I must announce to those who have no Godly influence or an influence that is corrupt, as well as to the Body of Christ, that TIME IS UP – and a shift is coming! To those who have been serving God with a passionate heart and without a lifestyle of compromise and have been pushed back into the corner of society for years by the ungodly, put a smile on your face – it's your time to reign now!

God is removing kings who are neither willing to heed the commandments of His Kingdom nor to listen to His instruction. I am not suggesting that the population of the Kingdom of God will regress at all; God's Kingdom has and never will be outnumbered. We are about to see more Kingdom people in places of influence than we have ever seen before. Things are shifting and God is going to have the final say. Child of God get ready to move into power!

This shifting of leadership is not only for the world but also for the Kingdom of God and the Body of Christ. To those people who have been in leadership positions within the Body of Christ and couldn't care less about what God wants or His Word – watch out – things are about to shift!

If you're a pastor who's just looking for a paycheck or allowing the people to run your church – watch out! A shift is coming! If you're a youth pastor and can't stay out of bed with your students – watch out! A shift is coming!

Your actions – or lack of actions – will cause God to strip you of your position of authority. Check out what happened to King Saul!

1 Samuel 15: 24-29 The Message Bible

24 Saul gave in and confessed, "I've sinned. I've trampled roughshod over GOD's Word and your instructions. I cared more about pleasing the people. I let them tell me what to do. 25 Oh, absolve me of my sin! Take my hand and lead me to the altar so I can worship GOD!"

26 But Samuel refused: "No, I can't come alongside you in this. You rejected GOD's command. Now GOD has rejected you as king over Israel."
27 As Samuel turned to leave, Saul grabbed at his priestly robe and a piece tore off.
28 Samuel said, "GOD has just now torn the kingdom from you, and handed it over to your neighbor, a better man than you are.
29 Israel's God-of-Glory doesn't deceive and he doesn't dither. He says what he means and means what he says."

Just as Saul found out, God will shift things on you. The Message Bible tells us that God says what He means and means what He says. He's taking positions of authority from people who have no desire to bring forth His Kingdom. Kingdoms are shifting, people are shifting, and things as we know them now are shifting.

I think that if there was ever anything that would cause God to shift things in the manner that He is, it's the fact that people either *waste* the gifts, talents and positions He has given them or they *abuse* them.

God will take from the one who is doing nothing with or abusing his position and give to one who is already multi-tasking and maximizing his or her gifts and authority – adding to their power of influence.

Here is another prime example of shifts and shifting that will be happening throughout the Body of Christ. As a matter of fact, it has already started. Let's consider an analogy Jesus used.

Matthew 25:14-29

14 Again, it will be like a man going on a journey, who called his servants and entrusted his property to them.
15 To one he gave five talents of money, to another two talents, and to another one talent, each according to his ability. Then he went on his journey.
16 The man who had received the five talents went at once and put his money to work and gained five more.
17 So also, the one with the two talents gained two more.
18 But the man who had received the one talent went off, dug a hole in the ground and hid his master's money.
19 After a long time the master of those servants returned and settled accounts with them.
20 The man who had received the five talents brought the other five. 'Master,' he said, 'you entrusted me with five talents. See, I have gained five more.'

21 His master replied, 'Well done, good and faithful servant! You have been faithful with a few things; I will put you in charge of many things. Come and share your master's happiness!'
22 The man with the two talents also came. 'Master,' he said, 'you entrusted me with two talents; see, I have gained two more.'
23 His master replied, 'Well done, good and faithful servant! You have been faithful with a few things; I will put you in charge of many things. Come and share your master's happiness!'
24 Then the man who had received the one talent came. 'Master,' he said, 'I knew that you are a hard man, harvesting where you have not sown and gathering where you have not scattered seed.
25 So I was afraid and went out and hid your talent in the ground. See, here is what belongs to you.'
26 His master replied, 'You wicked, lazy servant! So you knew that I harvest where I have not sown and gather where I have not scattered seed?
27 Well then, you should have put my money on deposit with the bankers, so that when I returned I would have received it back with interest.
28 "Take the talent from him and give it to the one who has the ten talents.
29 For everyone who has will be given more, and he will have an abundance. Whoever does not have, even what he has will be taken from him.

As I have stated before, time is up for people who are doing nothing but being a hindrance and holding up the blessings of God for people and regions. Time is up for people who constantly do nothing with what God has given to them. Time is up for lazy people who do not maximize the gifts and talents God has given to them. God is not so impressed that you have a gift or a talent, but He is impressed when you use it to its fullest potential. If you have been stagnant with what God has given you, start using your talents now or watch out – a shift is coming! If you're not sure what your talents may be, ask God to show you, but don't stop there; ask God how He would have you use them. I would also suggest that you take a spiritual gift analysis to help you pinpoint your talents and giftings.

Please understand me; I am not suggesting that God is looking to get rid of people. However, He is not going to let people with moods, attitudes, fears and unwillingness to move forward hold Him back from establishing His Kingdom here on earth.

Chapter One
Power Points

- ➢ **God is shifting positions of authority**

- ➢ **A kingdom is no greater than its king**

- ➢ **An unused gift or talent can easily be taken away**

Chapter Two

A Renewed Position of Authority

> The Body of Christ has been twisted, restricted and unable to extend its authority to change things and bring a Godly influence.

What I am about to release into your understanding, I truly believe, will change not only *your* life for the better, but also the lives of those for whom you possess the power of influence.

Influence is a powerful gift that God has given man and it holds the ability to impact lives forever. If there is one point I want to drive home with this book, it's this: The influence the Church started out with may have dramatically decreased over the years but now, not only is it being restored – it's about to shift. As I stated before, we have become more of a problem to society instead of being the answer. Jesus did not come to cause problems; instead, He came to fix them. The influence of the Church is being restored and bringing us to a place of predominance; things are shifting! There is a new day dawning; the wind of the Holy Ghost is beginning to blow as we have never experienced it before. God is shifting the power of the Church and the world's view of the Body of Christ. Soon it will no longer be the Church looking to the world for their approval and financial assistance, but the world coming to the Church for approval and answers. If there was ever a time to get happy, that time is now!

Over the next few chapters, I want to share with you more of the revelation God has shared with me concerning this prophetic word "shift" as it pertains to the Body of Christ. One of the main points of this revelation is about the man who was healed right in the middle of a Sabbath Day before a religious crowd.

Luke 6:6-10

6 On another Sabbath he went into the synagogue and was teaching, and a man was there whose right hand was shriveled.
7 The Pharisees and the teachers of the law were looking for a reason to accuse Jesus, so they watched him closely to see if he would heal on the Sabbath.
8 But Jesus knew what they were thinking and said to the man with the shriveled hand, "Get up and stand in front of everyone." So he got up and stood there.
9 Then Jesus said to them, "I ask you, which is lawful on the Sabbath: to do good or to do evil, to save life or to destroy it?"
10 He looked around at them all, and then said to the man, "Stretch out your hand." He did so, and his hand was completely restored.

Let's start with verse six. *"On another Sabbath he went into the synagogue and was teaching, and a man was there whose right hand was shriveled."*

I want you to note that it was not unusual for Jesus to go into the temple on the Sabbath; however, it was a big deal when He rocked the boat of religion. On this day, Jesus rocked – with vengeance – the boat of religion by openly breaking and superseding the Mosaic Law when He healed the man's hand.

I think it is important that you note it was his right hand that was shriveled and hindered, not his left. The Gospel of Mark recounts this event as well but does not reveal it was the man's right hand that was shriveled. You might be asking yourself, why does that make a difference? It makes a difference because throughout history, it has always been the right hand of a man that represents his authority.

Symbolically speaking, it is the right hand of a king/leader that carries the power to release blessings and impart authority. This is why Joseph became so upset that his father crossed his hands when blessing his sons, as was the custom to do before the older generation passed. Joseph knew well the symbolic power of the right hand. Typically, the blessing goes to the first born, but God switched things up by changing the order of the rights of the first born. This is a great example of the right hand blessing and authority.

Genesis 48:12-19 The Living Bible

12-13 Joseph took the boys by the hand, bowed deeply to him, and led the boys to their grandfather's knees – Ephraim at Israel's left hand and Manasseh at his right.

14 But Israel crossed his arms as he stretched them out to lay his hands upon the boys' heads, so that his right hand was upon the head of Ephraim, the younger boy, and his left hand was upon the head of Manasseh, the older. He did this purposely.

15 Then he blessed Joseph with this blessing: "May God, the God of my fathers Abraham and Isaac, the God who has shepherded me all my life, wonderfully bless these boys.

16 He is the Angel who has kept me from all harm. May these boys be an honor to my name and to the names of my fathers Abraham and Isaac; and may they become a mighty nation."

17 But Joseph was upset and displeased when he saw that his father had laid his right hand on Ephraim's head; so he lifted it to place it on Manasseh's head instead.

18 "No, Father," he said. "You've got your right hand on the wrong head! This one over here is the older. Put your right hand on him!"

19 But his father refused. "I know what I'm doing, my son," he said. "Manasseh too shall become a great nation, but his younger brother shall become even greater."

Even though Manasseh was the first born son, Israel's right hand was placed upon Ephraim's head during the releasing of the blessing of God from one generation to the next. Since the right hand was placed upon Ephraim's head, he became the recipient of the greater blessings.

One of the greatest symbols and points of this prophetic revelation is based on the condition of the right hand of the man in Luke, Chapter 6. I really like how the New International Readers Version states the condition of the hand; it says his hand was "twisted."

The right hand of the man in Luke, Chapter 6, is a representation of the status of the Body of Christ. For far too long, the Body has had a shriveled, dried-up, and restricted hand of authority. Before you disagree, let me clarify what I mean. I believe that sickness, poverty, impotent influence, and the inability to change things when authority has been given to do so are indications that our authority is twisted. **The Body of Christ has been twisted, restricted and unable to extend its authority to change things and bring a Godly influence.** Because we have not been exercising or functioning in our God-given authority, we have lost the power and force of our influence.

Due to this lack of authority and loss of influence, we, the Church, have blended in with the crowds just like that man in the synagogue. We have become the ones who have been pushed back into a corner of society. We have allowed the worldly systems to push us back – letting them call the shots – because we have become accustomed to our twisted, impotent form of authority and influence. But HOLD ON! I have good Gospel news! We're not at the end of the story – Jesus is getting ready to walk back into the temple like He did that day in Luke, Chapter 6, to set things in order and move us to the front! Brace yourself and get ready to see how Jesus is the Master at upbraiding religion and the traditions of men with undeniable acts of authority.

Chapter Two
Power Points

- **Influence is being restored back to the Body of Christ**

- **True authority is being restored back to the Body of Christ**

- **Jesus has zero tolerance toward the spirit and actions of religion**

Chapter Three

Ready, Set, Shift!

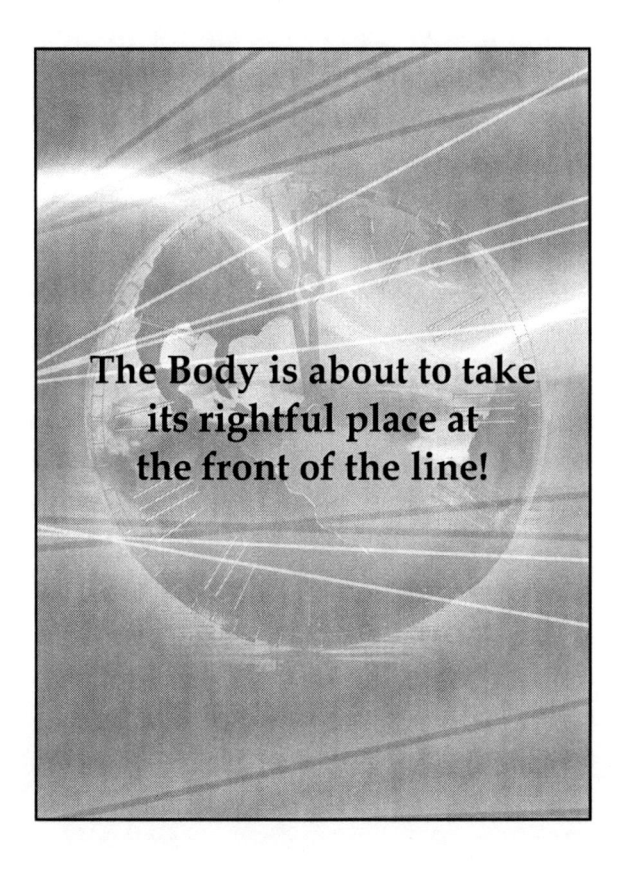

The Body is about to take its rightful place at the front of the line!

Luke 6:7-8

7 The Pharisees and the teachers of the law were looking for a reason to accuse Jesus, so they watched him closely to see if he would heal on the Sabbath.
8 But Jesus knew what they were thinking and said to the man with the shriveled hand, "Get up and stand in front of everyone." So he got up and stood there.

This section of Scripture shows that religiosity is basically everywhere – but the good news is Jesus is too! Here we see that the religious crowd is not only present but they are watching to see if, in fact, Jesus would break Mosaic Law and heal on the Sabbath Day or not. I am so thankful that He did!

In this next move and shifting of God, we will witness some of the greatest overthrows of tradition as people move with the flowing of the Holy Spirit. One of the primary changes to occur in the next shifting of the Holy Spirit will be "position."

Jesus did not condemn the man with the shriveled hand like most religious people would; instead, He just simply called him out. Jesus changed the man's position instantly. Verse 8 strongly suggests the man was located at the back of the crowd since Jesus asked him to stand out in front of everyone. He was called out of what was normal to him, which was being camouflaged by the swarming crowds of people in the synagogue. I want to bring out here that Jesus called the man with the twisted hand out of his comfort zone and hiding place. Basically, Jesus wanted him to be seen by all that were present in the synagogue that day.

Symbolically speaking, the Body has been so down-trodden and pushed to the back corner of the crowd of today's society that it has become comfortable for us to simply blend in instead of standing out front. I am here to tell you **the Body is about to take its rightful place at the front of the line!** We are about to shift from our place of no influence, no voice, no control, and no authority. Just as Jesus called that man out to the front, He is also calling us, the Body, to the front of the line.

God is shifting the Body of Christ right in the midst of a world that has been infiltrated with religiosity; that places the letter of the law and man-made religious practices above the Creator Himself and His Spirit. He's shifting us right in the midst of a world that has held the opinion and mindset that the Church is no more than a place for people who are of a lesser status in life or who are just plain ignorant.

God is moving the Body of Christ to the forefront of nations and to the forefront of the world. We are about to be restored to a place of visible authority right in front of this world that views the Body of Christ as a weak, unproductive bunch who lack even common sense. But, glory to God, there is a power shift coming to the Body as a whole and to your life personally!

This next move of God is going to put us back in control of the marketplace, back in control of the stock market, back in control of our schools, back in control of our governments, and in control of this planet! Right in the midst of all those people who mocked you and your God – calling you crippled and unproductive or something of that nature – get ready because things are shifting!

I am talking about full restoration – we're getting back our finances, our joy, our peace, our fight, our favor, and our power of influence! I believe that we are going to be put in such a place of influence that the world will come to us for financial assistance instead of us going to them! This world has been waiting for the full manifestation of the sons and daughters of God and they are about to see it.

It is important to state that we will never be able to successfully control, guide, and influence the world and the forces within it until we can successfully do so for ourselves. I know I could fill many pages on that statement alone, but that is not my assignment for this book. I believe that not everyone who wears a Christian label will be on the upside of this shifting – only those who are ready for the next move of God. On a personal level, this will be a very significant move.

You know that you have not always had it all together. You know that you have been subjected to the opinions of others. I am telling you, by the Holy Ghost, get ready to SHIFT! Get ready to get into alignment for your earthly assignment.

Chapter Three
Power Points

- ➢ We must break from religious ways and traditionalism in order to reach the next dimension of God

- ➢ God is moving us from our place of comfort to the assigned position He has for us

- ➢ This next shift is bringing not only full restoration to the Body, but also to us personally

Chapter Four

It's Time for MORE!

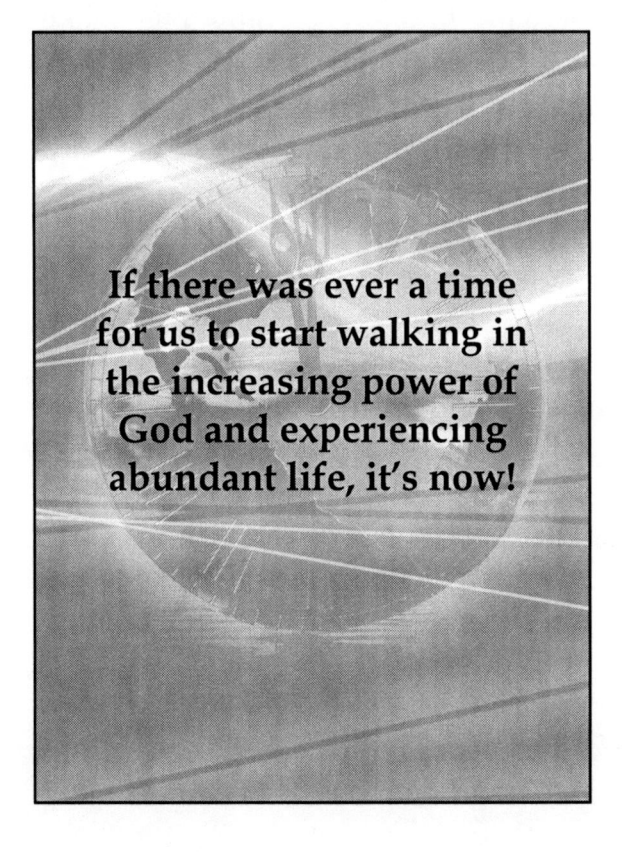

> If there was ever a time for us to start walking in the increasing power of God and experiencing abundant life, it's now!

The man with the shriveled hand was limited in his ability to function because of the condition of his hand. However, this lifestyle was *normal to him*. It was *normal* for him to wash and dress himself with the use of only one hand. It was *normal* for him to do chores and go about his day to day routine with the use of only one hand. It was *normal* for him to hold his wife and touch his children with the use of only one hand. The thought of having the use of both hands was nothing more than a dream. Let's face it; the man's limitation was simply just a way of life for him and all those around him.

I have to say this is also very true with the Body of Christ. We have put up with functioning within a lifestyle of limitation and thinking that it is *normal*. It's just *normal* to use second best items and hand-me-downs in the church due to a lack of funds. It's just *normal* to have bake sales in order to pay the electric bill or the rent for that month. It's just *normal* having to rob Peter to pay Paul. We have become content with functioning at less than our full potential.

We need to come out of functioning in and being comfortable with a lifestyle of limitations in every area of the Church – especially in the area of finances. Somebody reading this needs to make a decision and declaration right now that enough is enough and a limited lifestyle will no more be tolerated. I dare you to trust a limitless God and watch Him move you from a limited lifestyle to abundance.

Luke 6:10

He looked around at them all, and then said to the man, "Stretch out your hand." He did so, and his hand was completely restored.

This had to be one of the greatest days of that man's life. Jesus not only called this man out in front of everyone, but He fixed his problem. Jesus told the man to stretch forth his hand and when he did, it was restored!

Symbolically, not only is Jesus bringing us out in front for a position of influence, He is also restoring our authority (the right hand) so we can maintain our force of influence. Right in the midst of a world that has suppressed the Church, right in the midst of people who anticipated our failure (both corporately and personally); God is putting us back in control. I want to submit to you that not only did Jesus restore the man's confidence, position, influence, and authority, but He also gave the man the ability to get more! MORE! MORE! MORE! Jesus not only doubled this man's ability, He doubled his level of productivity – he got MORE!

If there was ever a time for us to start walking in the increasing power of God and experiencing abundant life, it's now!

In this next move of God and shifting of the Holy Spirit we, the Body, just like the man in Luke, Chapter 6, are going to double in all areas of our abilities, including the area of influence. No more will we have to submit to the ruling of the ungodly, having to rely on them to help us. God is putting us in a place of self-sufficiency (in Him). Oh, what an awesome thing it is to be self sufficient!

No longer will we have to look for hand-outs, and no longer will we have to rely on everyone else to help make ends meet. Wow – self sufficient and doubled all at the same time. Glory to God! Get ready to double! Get ready to increase! Get ready to have a greater force of influence in this world! We are coming into alignment for our assignment!

Here's what I am saying – it is time for Christians to stop being in the food stamp line and always looking for a hand-out. It's time to grow up, to mature and become self sufficient, to meet your own needs by faith in God. It's time for you to double your wealth. Some time ago, God spoke to me and said, "It is not increase that gets the world's attention, but it is wealth." Double your wealth! If you own a house, it's time for you to believe for two houses. If you're making $50,000 a year, it's time to believe for $100,000 a year. Go bigger! Go better! Go for the best! If you are living a life that is beneath, sub par, or not at the level of the promises of God – then that is not right. I challenge you to allow God to do what He did for that man in Luke, Chapter 6, and give you MORE! Jesus doubled that man's ability and productivity in an instant. What are you waiting for?

Let me break down what I am saying about personal wealth and increase. How can we expect to bless this world and be a blessing to the people who are in it without having any resources in our possession to do so? I believe that Christians should be in the position so that not only are their needs abundantly met, but they would also have the ability to meet the needs of the poor as well.

The people of this world are tired of the message of "Jesus loves you" without the work of Christ to back it up. Tell me how does shouting and proclaiming that "Jesus loves you" to people fill their stomach, or how does it clothe them? It takes money and wealth to convey the Gospel and to expand the Kingdom of God.

Wealth is coming in this next shifting of the Holy Spirit! It's coming to give us the upper hand so that we can influence this world for Christ. We have been made kings unto our God, and kings are made wealthy so they can support and expand the Kingdom. Kingdom expansion can only come by blessing others as God blesses you. Just think how great it would be to have the resources to pay off a single mother's debts or provide living quarters for a family in need. How great would it be for the Kingdom if we could just sell some land or transfer some funds to pay off our church's mortgage? Increase is coming to the Body of Christ to enable us to do the work of the Kingdom.

Not only is God moving the Body into a place of power and influence, He is also restoring our authority and giving us increase. He's going to give us double for our trouble! God is bringing us into *alignment* for our *assignment* to advance the Kingdom like never before.

The Bible says that "judgment must first start in the house of the Lord" (1 Peter 4:17 KJV). I like the way my pastor says it, "Judgment is not a bad thing, it just means to bring things into alignment."

This is exactly what took place with the man in Luke, Chapter 6. His twisted, shriveled, and hindered hand was brought into alignment so it could function and so he could fulfill his Godly assignment.

Chapter Four
Power Points

- ➢ We, the Body are moving from a position of limitation to a position of abundance

- ➢ We are about to be doubled

- ➢ We are moving from a lifestyle of second hand living to a lifestyle of self-sufficiency

Chapter Five

The All-At-Once Church

> **In this next shifting, God is aligning the Five Fold offices in their assignments.**

One of the paramount ways God will be bringing alignment to the Body is by the resurrection and restoration of the Five Fold Ministry offices – causing them to begin functioning in the Church once again. In Luke Chapter 6, not only did Jesus call that man out to the front of a religious bunch, but he also restored and revitalized his hand back to its proper position – just as if it had been that way all along.

Another great aspect of this story is that Jesus did more than restore the man's hand – He also restored the use of all the man's fingers – causing all five to work individually and together all at the same time. The symbolic part of the hand and this revelation is a very important element of this story because each finger represents a Five Fold Ministry office. The thumb represents the office of the "Apostle," which works with all of the other fingers/offices and has the ability to touch and be in contact with each of the other fingers/offices. If you were to make a fist you would see the thumb wraps all the other fingers and is the covering for them.

Next is the pointer finger, which represents the office of the "Prophet." A prophet is one who God uses to help point us in the right direction. You should always see the Apostle/thumb and the Prophet/pointer working together and in close proximity. Just look at your hand and see.

The middle finger is the longest finger on your hand, giving it the ability to reach out and extend beyond all the other fingers. The middle finger represents the office of the "Evangelist," who is the one who reaches out for lost souls. In looking at it you will also notice that it is the center finger, indicating that soul winning and evangelism should always be our center balance and core. The next finger in the line up is your ring finger, which represents the office of the "Pastor." He is the one who is married to the church and works closely with the Evangelist seeing that all the souls that are reaped have a place to go and an overseer to disciple them. The last finger on the hand is the pinky. The pinky is the support for all the other offices and it represents the office of the "Teacher." The teacher is the one who carries the ability to dig deep into the Bible and break it down for all to have a greater understanding.

In order to have a fully functioning hand, all five fingers must work individually and be able to work together as well. If you have a hand that moves around okay but the fingers don't function properly, you have a hand that is hindered, lacking power and strength.

You cannot fully control things in your hand if you have only a few fingers working. A hand that is limited in its ability is a hand that is in distress – and, therefore, the functioning fingers could suffer irreparable damage from having to over-compensate for the non-functioning fingers. The pointer finger can't do what the ring finger has been assigned to do and the thumb can't do what the pinky does because they have specific positions and abilities.

However, we can see this working in the Church today. We have teachers trying to be pastors and evangelists trying to be apostles and it's just not working because they are out of place.

People like this may be wondering why doors are not opening and there is no anointing on what they are doing – it's due to the simple fact that they are out of place and position!

God is only obligated to supply for the placement and position to where He calls you. Provision is always where the ordained position is. Let me help you – if you have been pastoring for ten years and you still have your same fifty people – you're probably not in the right office. You're trying to do something you've neither been assigned nor aligned to do. Now don't get me wrong, I am thankful for people who are doing things in the Body of Christ; Lord knows we need them. But let's do it right – let's get in to the right office, the right position, and the right calling. Let's get into correct alignment so that the life of God can flow!

In the next shifting of the Holy Ghost, we are going to see not only the resurrection and restoration of each of the Five Fold offices, but we will also see them working in the right position as well as working together. What an awesome thing it's going to be – the Five Fold Ministry gifts working all at the same time, all in the same place! We have had different movements throughout the Body – the evangelistic movement, the teaching movement, and the prophetic movement – but we have never had them all working at the same time and all under the same roof. There is going to be such a shift, such an influx of people into the local churches that it will be completely necessary to have all offices of the Five Fold Ministry working together just to keep things in order.

In this next shifting, God is aligning the Five Fold offices in their assignments. We already have living proof of that with the massive release of the apostolic anointing and the increased number of installed Apostles. This is very important because it will make way for the reestablishment of correct church government/five fold ministry offices in today's church and the church of tomorrow. One of the many benefits of having correct church government in place is so we can truly experience heaven on earth, because where His Word and His structure are – that is where we can find Him. Thy Kingdom come, thy will be done!

Chapter Five
Power Points

- ➢ **Restoration of all Five Fold Ministry offices within the local church**

- ➢ **Five Fold offices in support of each other and working all together**

- ➢ **Church government being restored and functioning as God has ordained it**

Chapter 6

The Breath of Revival

> I believe that we are getting into position and alignment for the greatest Holy Ghost explosion and out-pouring...

In this chapter, I want to share with you one of my personal beliefs. I know that there are those who will agree with me and others who may not, but I feel that I should share this with you. I believe that things are now starting to come into alignment with the restoration of the Body and the Five Fold Ministry and the power of our influence for a reason.

I believe that we are getting into position and alignment for the greatest Holy Ghost explosion and out-pouring, along with an acknowledgement of the Spirit of God, like we have not seen since the Book of Acts. Yes, they had the first out-pouring, and it was great, packed with power and flowing with unity. But it did not last. Today we see a Church that is far from the power, unity, and passion that was experienced at that time.

Now let's look at Ezekiel 37:4-10.

4 Then he said to me, "Prophesy to these bones and say to them, 'Dry bones, hear the word of the LORD!
5 This is what the Sovereign LORD says to these bones: I will make breath enter you, and you will come to life.
6 I will attach tendons to you and make flesh come upon you and cover you with skin; I will put breath in you, and you will come to life. Then you will know that I am the LORD.'"

7 So I prophesied as I was commanded. And as I was prophesying, there was a noise, a rattling sound, and the bones came together, bone to bone.
8 I looked, and tendons and flesh appeared on them and skin covered them, but there was no breath in them.
9 Then he said to me, "Prophesy to the breath; prophesy, son of man, and say to it, 'This is what the Sovereign LORD says: Come from the four winds, O breath, and breathe into these slain, that they may live.'
10 So I prophesied as he commanded me, and breath entered them; they came to life and stood up on their feet — a vast army.

I believe that the verses you have just read are key in helping us unlock revelation so we can experience this next out-pouring. I stated earlier that God is aligning us for the greatest out-pouring since the Book of Acts. But up to now, I believe that we have been limiting what God has wanted to do because we have not had the proper governmental structure in the Body. If you'll notice, God had Ezekiel call to the structure (bones) first, and then the tendons and the skin, and finally the wind. We have experienced great revivals over the years – and great manifestations of the Holy Spirit – but they have not remained with us. The wind has blown a little here and a little there – but that's just it – the wind blew in and then right back out.

I believe that we have not had a lasting revival and a major overflow of the power of God because there has been no structure to receive the wind and contain the wind, the breath of God. Before Ezekiel could call for the wind, he first had to have bones in place, but still it was not enough. The sinews, muscles and skin had to be present and in alignment in order for the army of men to be filled with the breath of God and function to its fullest ability. The problem today is we have preachers calling for the wind first when they should be calling for the structure to contain and sustain the wind.

The Five Fold Ministry offices are the main frame or structure (bones) of the local church. The sinew and muscles represent the leadership of the local church that works with the bones and helps make sure things are connected and flow smoothly. The skin is the membership of the local church, which serves to cover and protect the Five Fold and other positions of leadership represented in the church through the power of intercessory prayer. When they are all working together they will produce a great and mighty body/army for the Kingdom of God. This will allow the breath of God to continuously flow without ceasing.

One of the most important things we, as believers, can do is to flow with the shifting of God and be at the right place at the right time. God is a God of times and places. The Bible is full of examples of people who have been at the right place at the right time and people who have not. If that man in Luke, Chapter 6, had not shown up at the synagogue that day he would not have been restored.

God is a God of restoration and it's time to embrace the greatest shifting of the Holy Spirit that has ever happened; embrace the greatest alignment that has ever happened. Oh, let judgment and alignment begin at the House of the Lord!

Chapter Six
Power Points

- ➢ **The Body is being aligned for the greatest out-pouring of the Holy Spirit since the Day of Pentecost**

- ➢ **Structure will not only enable Gods plan for revival but will also maintain it**

- ➢ **We need to be open for the next move of God while keeping order in its place**

Chapter Seven

The Assignment

> As we come into alignment with this next major wave of shifts here on this earth, it will unlock heaven.

In the previous chapters I focused on how alignment is coming to the Body, but for this final chapter, I want to focus on the assignment and the reason for the alignment. Let me start by saying that this could be a very broad topic, but I would just like to deal with the area of Kingdom establishment and advancement. I am fully persuaded that God sent Jesus to re-establish the authority and influence that Adam lost in the Garden of Eden when he sinned before God. Some preachers say that Jesus gained back for humanity what Adam lost. This simply means that Jesus, by His death and resurrection, brought things back into alignment. He made a way for man to have access to heaven once again. It all goes back to the beginning and how God put man on this planet to manage it, walk in authority, and have dominion in every area and to have a great influence.

God is aligning the Body of Christ for our assignment and our assignment, in a nut shell, is to advance the Kingdom of God by the power and force of our influence. **As we come into alignment with this next major wave of shifts here on this earth, it will unlock heaven.** Our assignment is to unlock heaven in every ungodly situation that we encounter by the authority we have been given in Jesus. When we encounter sickness, we are to unlock healing. When we encounter poverty, we are to unlock prosperity.

When we encounter bondage, we are to unlock freedom. When we encounter religion, we are to bring relationship. We are to rise up as the sons of God and manifest His glory here in this earth.

Romans 8:19 Amplified Bible

19For [even the whole] creation (all nature) waits expectantly and longs earnestly for God's sons to be made known [waits for the revealing, the disclosing of their sonship].

I also like how the New Living Translation expresses the heart of God!

Romans 8:19 New Living Translation

19 For all creation is waiting eagerly for that future day when God will reveal who his children really are.

We are to rise up and move to the position to which God is calling us and to establish the Kingdom in every area of our lives and the lives of others. I believe that there are levels of God's glory that have not yet been released on this planet, but will be as we come in to this great alignment. Soon, and very soon, we shall see more and more of God's Kingdom being manifested as He calls us out to the forefront to reign in power. Simply put, the assignment at hand as God brings us into alignment is to manifest the Kingdom of God in greater ways than we have ever experienced before by the force of our influence.

As I close, I so much want to encourage you to embrace God and begin to follow the flow of the Holy Ghost. I am fully persuaded that God is beginning to speak to His people on different levels than He has before. Don't be afraid if you get asked to do something you have never heard of before, just run with it and do something you have never done before. You must realize that we are God's vehicles to bring His Kingdom to this generation and the next to come. It's time to not only live in – but release the miraculous!

Chapter Seven
Power Points

- ➢ God is aligning the Body to take over kingdoms and enforce His Kingdom here on this planet

- ➢ Alignment of the Body is key to opening the heavens over this earth so that we may show His glory

Closing Comments

In closing, I hope that this book has blessed you and created a new sense of hope and faith within you. God truly has a great future planned for you personally and for the Body as a whole. It is my intention to share with you that kings are truly shifting, the Five Fold Ministry is coming alive; and the Kingdom of God is being established through correct church government. I truly believe that our best days are ahead! Days of restored authority, days of being brought to the forefront, days of having more, and days of seeing more of God and the moving of His Spirit more than ever before!

May God bless you richly as you expand the Kingdom of God in your life.

Salvation

Maybe you have just finished this book and you don't know the Great Restorer, named Jesus Christ. Or maybe you once were in a relationship with Him and have walked away or simply gotten busy in life. No matter what your story may be, I know that you can have a greater finish by allowing Jesus to not only restore you, but also be your Savior and Lord. Please simply pray this prayer out loud so you can hear it with your own ears and mean it in your heart: Father God, I am a sinner and I need a Savior. I accept the victorious work Jesus did on the cross for me. I ask you now to wash me of all my sins and live in my heart, Lord Jesus. Amen.

Now begin to thank God for saving you and thank Him for restoring you back to life and life more abundantly. Thank you so much for allowing me to introduce you to my Savior, Jesus. I encourage you to get a Bible, find a great Bible preaching church, and walk in the best God has for you.

About the Author

Sean Walsh is a revelatory preacher who is fueled by a calling to Refresh, Restore, and Revolutionize the Body of Christ. A graduate of World Harvest Bible College, located in Columbus, Ohio, Sean offers years of leadership and true spiritual insight as he embraces the next move of God. Sean is a licensed minister, the founder of First Watch Ministries, and serves as CFO/COO at Strong Tower Ministries, located in Fredericksburg, Virginia, where he and his lovely wife, Kim, reside.

Additional Scriptural Examples of Kingdom Shifts

In this section, I want to highlight just a few of the many Kingdom shifts that are displayed throughout the Bible. It is exciting to know that God not only moved on behalf of mankind generations ago, but He still is doing so today.

It's Our Time to Reign!

Daniel 7:27

27 Then the sovereignty, power and greatness of the kingdoms under the whole heaven will be handed over to the saints, the people of the Most High. His kingdom will be an everlasting kingdom, and all rulers will worship and obey him.'

The Greatest Kingdom Shift of All Time; The Death and Resurrection of Jesus

Mark 15:25-16:7 King James Version

25 And it was the third hour, and they crucified him.
26 And the superscription of his accusation was written over, THE KING OF THE JEWS.
27 And with him they crucify two thieves; the one on his right hand, and the other on his left.
28 And the scripture was fulfilled, which saith, And he was numbered with the transgressors.
29 And they that passed by railed on him, wagging their heads, and saying, Ah, thou that destroyest the temple, and buildest it in three days,
30 Save thyself, and come down from the cross.
31 Likewise also the chief priests mocking said among themselves with the scribes, He saved others; himself he cannot save.
32 Let Christ the King of Israel descend now from the cross, that we may see and believe. And they that were crucified with him reviled him.
33 And when the sixth hour was come, there was darkness over the whole land until the ninth hour.
34 And at the ninth hour Jesus cried with a loud voice, saying, Eloi, Eloi, lama sabachthani? which is, being interpreted, My God, my God, why hast thou forsaken me?

35 *And some of them that stood by, when they heard it, said, Behold, he calleth Elias.*
36 *And one ran and filled a spunge full of vinegar, and put it on a reed, and gave him to drink, saying, Let alone; let us see whether Elias will come to take him down.*
37 *And Jesus cried with a loud voice, and gave up the ghost.*
38 *And the veil of the temple was rent in twain from the top to the bottom.*
39 *And when the centurion, which stood over against him, saw that he so cried out, and gave up the ghost, he said, Truly this man was the Son of God.*
40 *There were also women looking on afar off: among whom was Mary Magdalene, and Mary the mother of James the less and of Joses, and Salome;*
41 *(Who also, when he was in Galilee, followed him, and ministered unto him;) and many other women which came up with him unto Jerusalem.*
42 *And now when the even was come, because it was the preparation, that is, the day before the sabbath,*
43 *Joseph of Arimathaea, an honourable counsellor, which also waited for the kingdom of God, came, and went in boldly unto Pilate, and craved the body of Jesus.*
44 *And Pilate marvelled if he were already dead: and calling unto him the centurion, he asked him whether he had been any while dead.*

45 And when he knew it of the centurion, he gave the body to Joseph.
46 And he bought fine linen, and took him down, and wrapped him in the linen, and laid him in a sepulchre which was hewn out of a rock, and rolled a stone unto the door of the sepulchre.
47 And Mary Magdalene and Mary the mother of Joses beheld where he was laid.

Mark 16:1-7

1 And when the sabbath was past, Mary Magdalene, and Mary the mother of James, and Salome, had bought sweet spices, that they might come and anoint him.
2 And very early in the morning the first day of the week, they came unto the sepulchre at the rising of the sun.
3 And they said among themselves, Who shall roll us away the stone from the door of the sepulchre?
4 And when they looked, they saw that the stone was rolled away: for it was very great.
5 And entering into the sepulchre, they saw a young man sitting on the right side, clothed in a long white garment; and they were affrighted.
6 And he saith unto them, Be not affrighted: Ye seek Jesus of Nazareth, which was crucified: he is risen; he is not here: behold the place where they laid him.

7 But go your way, tell his disciples and Peter that he goeth before you into Galilee: there shall ye see him, as he said unto you.

King Solomon is Faced With a Kingdom Shift

1 Kings 11:1-13

1 King Solomon, however, loved many foreign women besides Pharaoh's daughter — Moabites, Ammonites, Edomites, Sidonians and Hittites.
2 They were from nations about which the LORD had told the Israelites, "You must not intermarry with them, because they will surely turn your hearts after their gods." Nevertheless, Solomon held fast to them in love.
3 He had seven hundred wives of royal birth and three hundred concubines, and his wives led him astray.
4 As Solomon grew old, his wives turned his heart after other gods, and his heart was not fully devoted to the LORD his God, as the heart of David his father had been.
5 He followed Ashtoreth the goddess of the Sidonians, and Molech the detestable god of the Ammonites.
6 So Solomon did evil in the eyes of the LORD; he did not follow the LORD completely, as David his father had done.
7 On a hill east of Jerusalem, Solomon built a high place for Chemosh the detestable god of Moab, and for Molech the detestable god of the Ammonites.

*8 He did the same for all his foreign wives, who burned incense and offered sacrifices to their gods.
9 The LORD became angry with Solomon because his heart had turned away from the LORD, the God of Israel, who had appeared to him twice.
10 Although he had forbidden Solomon to follow other gods, Solomon did not keep the LORD's command.
11 So the LORD said to Solomon, "Since this is your attitude and you have not kept my covenant and my decrees, which I commanded you, I will most certainly tear the kingdom away from you and give it to one of your subordinates.
12 Nevertheless, for the sake of David your father, I will not do it during your lifetime. I will tear it out of the hand of your son.
13 Yet I will not tear the whole kingdom from him, but will give him one tribe for the sake of David my servant and for the sake of Jerusalem, which I have chosen."*

Death of Moses

Joshua 1:1-5

1 After the death of Moses the servant of the LORD, the LORD said to Joshua son of Nun, Moses' aide:
2 "Moses my servant is dead. Now then, you and all these people, get ready to cross the Jordan River into the land I am about to give to them — to the Israelites.
3 I will give you every place where you set your foot, as I promised Moses.
4 Your territory will extend from the desert to Lebanon, and from the great river, the Euphrates — all the Hittite country — to the Great Sea on the west.
5 No one will be able to stand up against you all the days of your life. As I was with Moses, so I will be with you; I will never leave you nor forsake you.

Outpouring of the Holy Ghost

Acts 2:1-17

1 When the day of Pentecost came, they were all together in one place.
2 Suddenly a sound like the blowing of a violent wind came from heaven and filled the whole house where they were sitting.
3 They saw what seemed to be tongues of fire that separated and came to rest on each of them.
4 All of them were filled with the Holy Spirit and began to speak in other tongues as the Spirit enabled them.
5 Now there were staying in Jerusalem God-fearing Jews from every nation under heaven.
6 When they heard this sound, a crowd came together in bewilderment, because each one heard them speaking in his own language.
7 Utterly amazed, they asked: "Are not all these men who are speaking Galileans?
8 Then how is it that each of us hears them in his own native language?
9 Parthians, Medes and Elamites; residents of Mesopotamia, Judea and Cappadocia, Pontus and Asia,
10 Phrygia and Pamphylia, Egypt and the parts of Libya near Cyrene; visitors from Rome
11 (both Jews and converts to Judaism); Cretans and Arabs — we hear them declaring the wonders of God in our own tongues!"

12 Amazed and perplexed, they asked one another, "What does this mean?"
13 Some, however, made fun of them and said, "They have had too much wine."
14 Then Peter stood up with the Eleven, raised his voice and addressed the crowd: "Fellow Jews and all of you who live in Jerusalem, let me explain this to you; listen carefully to what I say.
15 These men are not drunk, as you suppose. It's only nine in the morning!
16 No, this is what was spoken by the prophet Joel:
17 In the last days, God says, I will pour out my Spirit on all people...

David Defeats Goliath

1 Samuel 17:40-50

40 Then he took his staff in his hand, chose five smooth stones from the stream, put them in the pouch of his shepherd's bag and, with his sling in his hand, approached the Philistine.
41 Meanwhile, the Philistine, with his shield bearer in front of him, kept coming closer to David.
42 He looked David over and saw that he was only a boy, ruddy and handsome, and he despised him.
43 He said to David, "Am I a dog, that you come at me with sticks?" And the Philistine cursed David by his gods.
44 "Come here," he said, "and I'll give your flesh to the birds of the air and the beasts of the field!"
45 David said to the Philistine, "You come against me with sword and spear and javelin, but I come against you in the name of the LORD Almighty, the God of the armies of Israel, whom you have defied.
46 This day the LORD will hand you over to me, and I'll strike you down and cut off your head. Today I will give the carcasses of the Philistine army to the birds of the air and the beasts of the earth, and the whole world will know that there is a God in Israel.
47 All those gathered here will know that it is not by sword or spear that the LORD saves; for the

battle is the LORD's, and he will give all of you into our hands."

48 As the Philistine moved closer to attack him, David ran quickly toward the battle line to meet him.

49 Reaching into his bag and taking out a stone, he slung it and struck the Philistine on the forehead. The stone sank into his forehead, and he fell facedown on the ground.

50 So David triumphed over the Philistine with a sling and a stone; without a sword in his hand he struck down the Philistine and killed him.

Jesus Heals a Man at the Pool of Bethesda

John 5:1-11 New Living Translation

1 Afterward Jesus returned to Jerusalem for one of the Jewish holy days.
2 Inside the city, near the Sheep Gate, was the pool of Bethesda, with five covered porches.
3-4 Crowds of sick people — blind, lame, or paralyzed — lay on the porches.
5 One of the men lying there had been sick for thirty-eight years.
6 When Jesus saw him and knew how long he had been ill, he asked him, "Would you like to get well?"
7 "I can't, sir," the sick man said, "for I have no one to help me into the pool when the water is stirred up. While I am trying to get there, someone else always gets in ahead of me."
8 Jesus told him, "Stand up, pick up your sleeping mat, and walk!"
9 Instantly, the man was healed! He rolled up the mat and began walking! But this miracle happened on the Sabbath day.
10 So the Jewish leaders objected. They said to the man who was cured, "You can't work on the Sabbath! It's illegal to carry that sleeping mat!"
11 He replied, "The man who healed me said to me, 'Pick up your sleeping mat and walk.'"

Waters of Jericho Healed

2 Kings 2:19-21 King James Version

19 And the men of the city said unto Elisha, Behold, I pray thee, the situation of this city is pleasant, as my lord seeth: but the water is naught, and the ground barren.
20 And he said, Bring me a new cruse, and put salt therein. And they brought it to him.
21 And he went forth unto the spring of the waters, and cast the salt in there, and said, Thus saith the LORD, I have healed these waters; there shall not be from thence any more death or barren land.

Walls of Jericho Fall

Joshua 6:1-5

1 Now Jericho was tightly shut up because of the Israelites. No one went out and no one came in.
2 Then the LORD said to Joshua, "See, I have delivered Jericho into your hands, along with its king and its fighting men.
3 March around the city once with all the armed men. Do this for six days.
4 Have seven priests carry trumpets of rams' horns in front of the ark. On the seventh day, march around the city seven times, with the priests blowing the trumpets.
5 When you hear them sound a long blast on the trumpets, have all the people give a loud shout; then the wall of the city will collapse and the people will go up, every man straight in."

Elijah Calls Down Fire from Heaven

1 Kings 18:26-38

26 So they took the bull given them and prepared it. Then they called on the name of Baal from morning till noon. "O Baal, answer us!" they shouted. But there was no response; no one answered. And they danced around the altar they had made.
27 At noon Elijah began to taunt them. "Shout louder!" he said. "Surely he is a god! Perhaps he is deep in thought, or busy, or traveling. Maybe he is sleeping and must be awakened."
28 So they shouted louder and slashed themselves with swords and spears, as was their custom, until their blood flowed.
29 Midday passed, and they continued their frantic prophesying until the time for the evening sacrifice. But there was no response, no one answered, no one paid attention.
30 Then Elijah said to all the people, "Come here to me." They came to him, and he repaired the altar of the LORD, which was in ruins.
31 Elijah took twelve stones, one for each of the tribes descended from Jacob, to whom the word of the LORD had come, saying, "Your name shall be Israel."
32 With the stones he built an altar in the name of the LORD, and he dug a trench around it large enough to hold two seahs of seed.

33 He arranged the wood, cut the bull into pieces and laid it on the wood. Then he said to them, "Fill four large jars with water and pour it on the offering and on the wood."
34 "Do it again," he said, and they did it again. "Do it a third time," he ordered, and they did it the third time.
35 The water ran down around the altar and even filled the trench.
36 At the time of sacrifice, the prophet Elijah stepped forward and prayed: "O LORD, God of Abraham, Isaac and Israel, let it be known today that you are God in Israel and that I am your servant and have done all these things at your command.
37 Answer me, O LORD, answer me, so these people will know that you, O LORD, are God, and that you are turning their hearts back again."
38 Then the fire of the LORD fell and burned up the sacrifice, the wood, the stones and the soil, and also licked up the water in the trench.

Lazarus Raised From the Dead

John 11:38-44

38 Jesus, once more deeply moved, came to the tomb. It was a cave with a stone laid across the entrance.
39 "Take away the stone," he said. "But, Lord," said Martha, the sister of the dead man, "by this time there is a bad odor, for he has been there four days."
40 Then Jesus said, "Did I not tell you that if you believed, you would see the glory of God?"
41 So they took away the stone. Then Jesus looked up and said, "Father, I thank you that you have heard me.
42 I knew that you always hear me, but I said this for the benefit of the people standing here, that they may believe that you sent me."
43 When he had said this, Jesus called in a loud voice, "Lazarus, come out!"
44 The dead man came out, his hands and feet wrapped with strips of linen, and a cloth around his face. Jesus said to them, "Take off the grave clothes and let him go."

To purchase more resources please visit us at
www.firstwatchministries.com

If you are interested in booking information for:

Special events
Conferences
Revival meetings
Motivational speaking

Please contact us at www.firstwatchministries.com

First Watch Ministries
PO Box 446
Fredericksburg, Virginia 22404

www.firstwatchministries.com

Notes

Notes

Notes

Notes

Notes

Notes

Notes

Notes